# MAY I INTRODUCE YOU TO THE MESSAGE OF CHRISTIANITY?

Earl M. Blackburn

## VERITAS HERITAGE PRESS
VERITAS HERITAGE PRESS
173 Brook Hill Court, Elkin, NC, 28621, USA

\*

*Copyright © 2024 by Earl M. Blackburn*
*All rights reserved.*

ISBN-13: 978-1-7375898-7-7

Typeset in Dante Figures

Cover Design & Typesetting: Caleb A. Blackburn
Cover Design: A and Ω are the first and last respective letters of the Greek alphabet. They represent the totality of all that God is and what should be believed about him (see Isaiah 44:6; Revelation 1:8 & 22:13).

Printed by
Kindle Direct Publishing
Additional Copies May be Purchased at Amazon.com

"If religious books are not widely circulated among the masses in this country, I do not know what is going to become of us as a nation. If truth be not diffused, then error will be. If God and His Word are not known and received, the devil and his works will gain the ascendency. If the evangelical volume does not reach every hamlet, the pages of a corrupt and licentious literature will. If the power of the gospel is not felt throughout the length and breadth of this land, anarchy and misrule, degradation and misery, corruption and darkness will reign without mitigation or end." -Daniel Webster- (c. 1823)

## *The Foundations Series*

*The Foundations Series is governed by Psalm 11:3, "If the foundations be destroyed, what can the righteous do?" This series is a return to the foundational truths of biblical and historic Christianity, to inform the minds, warm the hearts, and motivate the wills of all who read.*

# Preface

Luke, the human writer of the third book of the New Testament, did something interesting. He was a Gentile (the only non-Jewish writer of the New Testament) and a man of medical science, a doctor. Initially, he was not a believer in Jesus, but having heard the reports about Him set out to investigate matters. (Interestingly, most who hear never investigate.) His investigation brought him into contact with those who were with Jesus from the beginning and who "from the beginning were eyewitnesses and ministers of the Word" of all these things (see 1 Corinthians 15:5-8). Upon hearing testimony and reports of those who were actually there, he came to saving faith in Jesus as the Christ, who became his Lord and Savior. Afterwards, he wrote a narrative of "those things which are most surely believed among us" (see Luke 1:1-4), universally known as *The Gospel According to Luke*. Luke's pattern is the investigative model I want to use in introducing you to the message of Christianity.

**Earl M. Blackburn,** *Pastor Emeritus*
Elkin, North Carolina
February 14th, 2024

# May I Introduce You to the Message of Christianity?

## Christianity – A Religion

In this day, the world of humanity is fractured, divided by its many ethnicities, languages, cultures, social strata, philosophies, ideologies, social agendas, religions, creeds, and core beliefs. This is especially true when it comes to religions and faith systems. According to *Adherents,* an independent, non-religiously affiliated organization that monitors the number and size of the world's religions, there are some 4,300 religions in the world. Without giving a definition of what constitutes a religion, the *Adherents* statisticians divide religions into churches, denominations, congregations, religious bodies, faith groups, tribes, cultures, and movements. All are of varying size and influence, with some being only a handful of people.

According to a recent and reasonably accurate census, the twenty most widely practiced religions of the world are as follows:

1. Christianity (2.1 billion)
2. Islam (1.3 billion)
3. Nonreligious (e.g., Secular/Agnostic/Atheist) (1.1 billion)
4. Hinduism (900 million)
5. Chinese traditional religions (e.g., Confucianism, Han, Taoism – 394 million)
6. Buddhism (376 million)
7. Primal-indigenous (300 million)
8. African traditional and Diasporic (100 million)

9. Sikhism (23 million)
10. Juche (19 million, almost exclusively in North Korea)
11. Spiritism (15 million)
12. Judaism (14 million)
13. Bahai (7 million)
14. Jainism (4.2 million)
15. Shinto (4 million)
16. Cao Dai (4 million)
17. Zoroastrianism (2.6 million)
18. Tenrikyo (2 million)
19. Neo-Paganism (1 million)
20. Unitarian-Universalism (800,000)[1]

Twelve of these are considered classical world religions—those religions most often studied in world religion classes and included in history of world religion surveys. They are Baha'i, Buddhism, Christianity, Confucianism, Hinduism, Islam, Jainism, Judaism, Shinto, Sikhism, Taoism, and Zoroastrianism.

A few of these religions are unfamiliar and some are more well-known in Western civilization, but most are completely unknown. The purpose of this short book is *not* to explore, compare, discuss and debate, nor to praise and ridicule the merits and demerits of each religion. Instead, it is to communicate in a clear and positive way the basic overall message of Christianity, the largest of the world's religions, and to present it in a simple and clear manner so that you will understand it. Also, to be candid with the reader, there is a secondary purpose. Upon understanding the basic message of

---

[1] This information was collected from
https://www.theregister.co.uk/2006/10/06/the_odd_body_religion/.
Accessed: 01/03/2019.

Christianity, it is hoped that you will become a true and earnest Christian.

It should be carefully noted before we begin that *not* one of the world's religions (contrary to popular thinking) is a unified and monolithic structure. Each religion has branches, categories, groups, and subgroups within the groups. Non-religious people and devotees of every religion would like to think that each religion is completely uniform and without seams or divisions. That is an idealist view but not a realistic one. Like all of the religions of the world, Christianity has branches and subgroups. The three major branches of Christianity are Roman Catholicism, Eastern Orthodoxy, and Protestantism, each containing subgroups too numerous to examine. The various branches within Catholicism are usually called orders; within Eastern Orthodoxy they are usually called communities, and within Protestantism they are usually called denominations. This is not meant to include those considered unorthodox by historic Christianity (e.g., Rosicrucianism, Jehovah's Witnesses, Mormons, Shepherd's Chapel, to name few).

Unlike animals, humans are deeply religious – including those who claim to be atheists. Everybody worships something, even if it is not God or some other deity. Worship is being engaged in and passionately practiced by almost everyone about something every day, whether it is political ideologies, social justice activism, hobbies, educational achievements, environmental causes, pleasure pursuits, sports, or you name it. A classic example is the average Saturday or Sunday in the United States. On those days, people attend more athletic stadiums or sporting arenas than they do churches or synagogues. (This does not include those who watch the events on television.) They clap and cheer, yell and scream, chant slogans, boo or celebrate the players, and verbally agree or disagree with the officials as they "pull" for their team. There are flags and banners, music and bands, and mascots and pep/cheer leaders to excite the crowd. Without even realizing it, they are engaged in a form of worship. Observe the "fans" (short for "fanatic") and you will see their religious fervor. Understand that even the person who does not believe in God has a religion. It can be the Temple of Reason, the Cathedral of Modern Science, the Basilica of Self, or the Shrine of Atheism. Some of the most religious people I've ever seen are atheists; they are passionate about their atheism. Unless a person is comatose, something drives and excites everyone. Why do I make such an audacious claim that humans are deeply religious? Because God Almighty, the Creator of heaven and earth, made each person with an immortal soul, a God-consciousness. If you do not worship God, you will find something else to worship and in which to invest devotional or religious time and energy!

One final thing before you read any further: If you have a Holy Bible, please keep it beside you so you can look up the plethora of Scripture references that will be given throughout this study. If you do not have a Holy Bible, borrow or buy one. Bibles are readily available.[2]

---

[2] Although the Holy Bible is officially banned in fifty-five countries around the world, it is easily obtained.

# A Brief Survey of Christianity's Beginnings

Who is a Christian, or what is Christianity? Randomly ask fifty different people and you might get as many different answers. Historic biblical and theological terms, which once were precise and well-known, have now become so generally nondescript that people seldom think about them or consider what a Christian or Christianity may actually be. People usually become satisfied with undefined terms and vague descriptions. Nominalism has set in!

To answer the question of what Christianity is, or who is a Christian, you need to strip away the various denominational identities and trappings and start at the beginning. Where did it start and how did it all begin? You must return to a study of its point of origin and to its primary source document, the Holy Bible. (This point will be developed later.)

## Some Aspects About Christianity

Each religion has certain characteristics and makes distinctive claims about itself. And, why not? It's understandable since each wants others to believe and benefit from its ideas. I will never forget visiting the Shwedagon Pagoda, also known as the Golden Pagoda, located in Yangon, Myanmar (formerly Rangoon, Burma). It is claimed to be, and perhaps is, the oldest Buddhist pagoda in the world. While touring clockwise the gold-covered domed pagoda and its massive complex, I noticed in one of the porticos an enthusiastic monk preaching. Although I did not understand a single Burmese word he said, he so caught my attention by his spirited animation that I asked my Burmese pastor friend to translate what the monk was saying. The translator said he was chastising his listeners for not believing more seriously Buddha's teachings and not being more devout, and he was making some unusual assertions about the meaning of life, suffering, and contentment. I thought to myself, *Hmmm, very interesting, not unlike many Baptists, Methodists, Catholics, and Muslims I know.*

Historic Christianity, too, has distinct and unusual aspects and claims about itself.[3] Since time and space forbid a full explanation of each, we'll discuss them briefly. Christianity is a supernatural religion, as opposed to a natural one. It did not emerge and evolve as a process of natural and humanistic thinking. Instead, it was birthed by divine and supernatural revelation and grew by sovereign power. It proclaims a glorious, absolutely almighty God, who is unlike any other god (so-called). It provides the only logical and rational answer to all the evil and wrongs in the world. It gives explanation to all the problems and failures of ancient Israel and why there is continual turmoil in the Middle East. It sheds light upon all the rituals and animal sacrifices of the Old Testament. It is the foundation of the Old Testament prophet's message. It centers on the most unique person who has ever been born and lived (Jesus Christ). It focuses on the most unusual work ever to be

---

[3] I wish to make a distinction between historic apostolic and orthodox Christianity, which originated with Jesus and His apostles, and much of modern Liberal Christianity, which has departed from many of the original teachings of the early church and has evolved into a quasi-moralistic social club. Most early Christians would not recognize large sections of modern Christianity. For further study on this current departure and phenomena, see *Christianity and Liberalism*, by J. Gresham Machen (London: Victory Press, 1923; new ed. Grand Rapids, Michigan: Wm. B. Eerdmans Publishing Co. 2009). This book is 100 years old, but it seems like it was written yesterday.

performed: the crucifixion, resurrection, and ascension into heaven of Jesus Christ. It offers the most perplexing, and simultaneously, the most powerful tidings in all the world (the gospel). It bestows the most priceless benefits imaginable (love, peace, joy, forgiveness, meaning, fulfillment, etc.) It demands from God a twofold response from all those who hear the message (repentance and faith). It erects a dynamic yet simple ecclesiastical structure. It produces a transformative ethic and view of life and work. It contains certain, wonderful, and almost unbelievable promises. It sets forth some of the most terrible and fearful warnings. It declares a final and righteous resolution to all the world's conflicts and problems. Supremely, it is all about the revelation, glory, and vindication of the true and living God in human history and life. Several biblical passages illustrate this final point:

Ephesians 3:20-21: *²⁰ Now unto him who is able to do exceedingly abundantly above all that we ask or think, according to the power at worketh in us, ²¹ Unto him be glory in the church by Christ Jesus throughout all ages, world without end. Amen.*

Romans 11:33-36: *³³ O the depth of the riches and wisdom and knowledge of God! How unsearchable are his judgments, and his ways past finding out! ³⁴ "For who hath known the mind of the Lord? or who hath been his counselor?" ³⁵ "Or who hath given [a gift] to him that he might be repaid?" ³⁶ For of him, and through him and to him are all things: to him be glory forever. Amen.*

2 Corinthians 4:3-6: *³ But if our gospel be hid, it is hid to them that are lost. ⁴ In whom the god of this world hath blinded the minds of them which believe not, lest the light of the glorious gospel of Christ, who is the image of God, should shine unto them. ⁵ For we preach not ourselves, but Christ Jesus the Lord; and ourselves your servants for*

*Jesus' sake. ⁶For God, who commanded the light to shine out of darkness, hath shined in our hearts, to give the light of the knowledge of the glory of God in the face of Jesus Christ.*

## What is the Message of Christianity?

Christianity is an established religion and statistically the world's largest. It bears all the marks of a religion, but it is much more than just another religion. For many who have *not* studied the Bible, allow me to tell you a few things it is *not*. Christianity is not simply about being and doing good, treating others as one would like to be treated, having some type of religious experience, being baptized, giving money to the church and charitable causes, doing good deeds with the hope of earning entrance into Heaven, being happy or healthy or rich, having good self-esteem, or even being part of a church (although, the church is the indispensable structural foundation of Christianity), Christianity is much more than a person being a part of a church. Going to church does not make one a Christian any more than going to a zoo makes one a lion or swimming in the ocean makes one a fish. Christianity's essence is a *unique* message and belief system that produces a *distinct* lifestyle.

Yet, the question remains, "What is its message?" Many answers have been given throughout the centuries by religious scholars, secular historians, philosophers, and sociologists. Some answers are complex and others are simple. Some scholars are opponents and others are defenders. This book is a humble attempt to help you cut through the extraneous brush of complexities and come to a simple understanding of historic, apostolic, and orthodox Christianity. Rather than filtering through two thousand years of Christian history and tradition, let us go back to the days of yesteryear and start at the point of origin. To do this we must return to the primary source of the Christian faith – the Holy Bible. Rather than using one verse or passage of the Holy Scriptures, I will draw from the entire Bible to discover the answer. You must see the entire forest before you study the individual trees. (Note carefully: Although some verses will be incorporated in the main body of writing, most Scripture references will be given in the footnotes for each point.)

## Christianity Begins with A Book

While the Holy Bible begins with God (see Genesis 1:1), Christianity is founded upon the Holy Bible. Without the Book of books – the Holy Bible – there would be no Christianity or saving knowledge of God! University of Edinburgh Emeritus Professor Larry W. Hurtado notes that most people today think that the ancient religions had sacred books or texts which were central to their religious foundations. However, when a wider and deeper study is made of religions through the ages, it will be discovered that is not the case. Until the last two millennia, almost all ancient religions were based on and communicated by oral tradition and ritual or ceremony. There existed no written directives of beliefs and practices. Conversely, and according to Professor Hurtado, Christianity was a "bookish" religion:

> I simply assert that reading, writing, copying, and dissemination of texts had a major place – indeed, a prominence – in early Christianity that, except for ancient Jewish circles, was unusual for religious groups in the Roman era…Other scholars also have referred to early

Christian circles as 'constitutionally oriented to texts' and as 'textual communities' and have described the early Christian movement collectively as one with 'texts at its very heart and soul.'[4]

In other words, Christianity is *not* based upon oral tradition or established ritual (as almost all other religions, Judaism excepted), but upon proven and time-honored written documents from the original sources, such as prophets and apostles. These documents are the Hebrew Old Testament and the Greek New Testament (collectively known as the Holy Bible) and are the primary source foundations for authentic Christianity.[5] It is to this book that you must turn if you are to understand the message of Christianity!

Every person has a presupposition. For example, everyone presupposes that a Rolls Royce is an excellent automobile because of its antiquity, quality, beauty, luxury, and price. We Christians, likewise, have a presupposition from which we start all our discussions. We presuppose the Holy Bible is the very Word of the living God that He revealed from heaven about Himself.[6] This presupposition leads to the great question,

---

[4] *Destroyer of the gods: Early Christian Distinctiveness in the Roman World* (Baylor University Press: Waco, Texas, 2016) 105-106.

[5] Hinduism followed the pattern of Judaism's Old Testament with the Bhagavad Gita (c. 200 BC-AD 200). Buddhism followed the same pattern with the Gandharan Scrolls (c. 100 BC-AD 300) and Islam copied the pattern of Christianity in the 7th century AD with the publishing of the Koran (Qu,ran), between the years of AD 610-632. Note carefully: the earliest parts of the Hebrew Old Testament (the Torah) predated all other religious writings by approximately 2,000 years!

[6] See *May I Introduce You to the Holy Bible*, Earl M. Blackburn (Elkin, North Carolina: Veritas Heritage Press, 2021).

"How can people really and truly come to know God and understand life around them?"

While philosophers and religious leaders have wrestled with this question for millennia, the average person is not immune to this struggle. Many face this question daily in hospitals, at the scenes of tragic accidents, or when life's unexpected calamities flip them head over heels. It is sometimes heard "Is there a God?" Or "If there is a God, why did this happen and why did it happen now? I never saw it coming." Also, "If there is a God, how can I know Him personally?"

Thus, since the emergence of Christianity, almost all religions have developed some type of sacred writing that seeks to help people know or better understand their god, or to understand their belief and practices. Yet, we are taught that *"the world through wisdom did not know God"* (1 Corinthians 1:21). I can hear you say, "What? You mean human reasoning and natural intellect, coupled with philosophical theories and scientific presuppositions, with all their (supposed) cleverness and intuitive skills, *cannot* discover or even know God?" Yes, that is exactly what I am saying. Totally unreliable are our own emotions and feelings, which can fluctuate on a day-to-day, or even on an hour-to-hour basis. Despite the failures and deficiencies of natural intellect, advanced human reasoning, vacillating human feelings, and speculative progresses in modern science, we are *not* left to grope in the dark. The Lord God, the Creator, reminds us of His own superior wisdom and thinking and instructs us to look beyond ourselves to Him: *"For my thoughts are not your thoughts, neither are your ways my ways, saith the LORD. For as the heavens are higher than the earth, so are my ways higher than your ways, and my thoughts than your thoughts"* (Isaiah 55:8-9).

God, indeed, has spoken since creation and continues to speak to His world to this very day. Still, you may ask, "How then does God speak to us today? How does He communicate who He is, what is true and false, what He has done, what is His will, what He requires of us, and what He will ultimately do?" He does *not* do so with fickle feelings that change from day to day, nor with mystical audible voices, nor with our own speculative and unstudied thoughts, nor with cultural concepts that may be prevalent at a given point in human history. God unmistakably and steadily communicates today in a book. This book, which is the self-revelation of God, is the Holy Scriptures. The Holy Bible is the Book of books and is inspired by God. It is inerrant, authoritative, infallible, clear, preserved, and sufficient for anything that anyone faces. This is what Paul the Apostle meant when he said in 2 Timothy 3:16, *"All Scripture is given by **inspiration** of God, and is profitable for doctrine, for reproof, for correction, for instruction in righteousness."*[7]

What Jesus said in rebuke to the religious leaders of His day is also true of the multitudes of our day: *"Ye do err, not knowing the Scriptures, nor the power of God"* (Matthew 22:29). This rebuke contains two fatal flaws of non-Christians and nominal Christians, alike. These two fatal flaws have pervaded the last two thousand years: 1) people do *not* know the Scriptures, and

---

[7] The word inspiration is the Greek word *theopneustos* – θεόπνευστος, which literally means God breathed out. In inspiration, God breathed out His Word into human authors and they wrote down His words directly communicated from Him to them, by the Holy Spirit (see 2 Peter 1:20-21).

2) they do not know the power of God. This lack of knowledge is both intellectual and experiential (i.e., experienced).

Again, as Professor Hurtado so powerfully states it: "Any adequate analysis of early Christianity must reckon with its 'bookish' nature…In short, 'textuality' was central, and, from the outset, early Christianity was, indeed, 'a bookish religion'."[8]

The following has aptly been said:

> The Holy Bible contains the mind of God, the state of man, the way of salvation, the doom of sinners, and the happiness of believers. Its doctrines are holy, its precepts are binding, its histories are true, and its decisions are immutable. Read it to be wise, believe it to be safe, and practice it to be holy. It contains light to direct you, spiritual food to support you, and comfort to cheer you. It is the traveler's map, the pilgrim's staff, the pilot's compass, the soldier's sword, heaven opened, and the gates of hell disclosed. Christ is its grand object, our good its design, and the glory of God its end. It should fill the memory, rule the heart, and guide the feet. Read it slowly, frequently, and prayerfully. It is a mine of wealth, a paradise of glory, and a river of pleasure. It is given you in life, shall be opened in judgment, and will be remembered forever. It involves the highest responsibilities, will reward the greatest labor, and will condemn all who trifle with its sacred contents *(Gideons International)*.

---

[8] *Destroyer of the gods: Early Christian Distinctiveness in the Roman World.* 141.

Consequently, Christianity's message, though primarily and most importantly is about God, its foundation does not begin directly with God. Instead, it begins with the written Word of God, the Holy Bible, which is the self-disclosure and self-revelation of God Himself to the world of humanity. While God generally reveals Himself in creation and in the human conscience, He specifically and especially reveals Himself in the Holy Bible, His Word. Furthermore, His Word unfolds God's grandeur through His marvelous redemptive acts and works, especially the works of Jesus. John, the beloved Apostle, concludes the fourth Gospel with this testimony: *"And there are also many other things which Jesus did, the which, if they should be written every one [lit. one by one], I suppose that even the world itself could not contain the books that would be written. Amen"* (John 21:25).

Again, take careful note that without the Holy Bible there would be no Christianity! Furthermore, a person cannot pick and choose what he likes or dislikes, embrace the perceived good portions and reject the imagined bad portions. The Holy Bible must be taken as a whole, as it was intended, and not parceled out according to tastes and preferences. Thus, the true and living God, God Almighty, cannot be savingly and personally known unless you know the Holy Scriptures!

## Who is God?

What or who is God? Professor J.I. Packer notes, "Many say they believe in God, but have no idea who it is they believe in, or what difference believing in Him may make."[9] Since the

---

[9] J.I. Packer, *Knowing God* (InterVarsity Press: Downers Grove, Illinois, 1973) 143.

subtle invasion of German "higher critical thinking" into the Western world (especially the United States), in the middle of the 1800s, the biblical teaching of God has been subtly distorted. People who say they believe in God have little idea of who He is. When you think of God, what comes to mind? Is He a heavenly being only slightly bigger and better than yourself or one altogether like yourself? Is He a celestial Santa Claus or a sweet Grandpa, who is there to pat your head and give you whatever your heart desires? Is He a kind and gentlemanly old man that wants to do things in the earth, but is powerless to do so because He is constantly thwarted by the forceful actions of people in the world? Or is He the Almighty, who sits in the heavens and does whatsoever He pleases (see Psalm 115:3)? Professor Packer makes the following pointed observation:

> We are modern men, and modern men, though they cherish great thoughts of man, have as a rule small thoughts about God. When the man in the Church, let alone the man in the street, uses the word 'God,' the thought in his mind is rarely of divine *majesty*.[10]

The major problem in the Christian Church today, and especially among people in the world, is that their thoughts of God are *too* small. Slight, weak, timid, indecisive, frustrated, constantly changing to accommodate rapidly evolving societies, loving, and wanting to help but powerless are often the concepts that linger in the backs of the average person's mind. However, when you turn to the Holy Scriptures, a totally different picture emerges.

---

[10] *Knowing God*, 73-74.

Who, then, is God and what does the Holy Bible teach us about Him? What is He like? Are there many gods? Are the gods of different religions the one and same God, only using different names? There is a familiar saying that was derived from the ancient Roman Empire: "All roads lead to Rome." Many modern people have taken this saying and asked these questions: *"Do not all religions lead to God and heaven?" "Are not all religions basically the same and equal?"* Biblical and historic Christianity is quick to answer: *No!* Others might think, *"Does it really matter what god or religion a person believes so long as the person is sincere and good?"* Again, orthodox Christianity speedily answers: *Yes, it does really matter not only now, but for all eternity!*

Furthermore, there is something that is important to understand and remember. God does not reveal the truths about Himself at one time in one place but scatters the truths about Himself throughout the entirety of Holy Scripture, from Genesis to Revelation. Contrary to the modern-day fixation of wanting everything quick and easy, the rich and rewarding truths about God do not come to the lazy and sleepy reader, who does not wish to spend time and effort in careful study. Instead, the truths about God come through a diligent and attentive reading of the entire Bible. What then do the Scriptures teach about God? Let us consider the progressively and redemptively revealed truths found throughout the entirety of the Word of God.

## There is only one God

The Holy Bible is quite clear: there is only one God, not many! Scripture opens its sacred pages with the first words of an emphatic declaration: *"In the beginning God..."* (Genesis 1:1), as opposed to many gods. Later, God declares to Israel in what is known as the *Shema, "Hear, O Israel: The LORD our God is one LORD"* (Deuteronomy 6:4). \*In Mark 12:28-34, Jesus affirmed this truth in His encounter with a Jewish scribe. While many verses could be found and are used throughout the Bible to verify this truth, a few will suffice:

Isaiah 44:6, *"Thus saith the Lord the King of Israel, and his redeemer the Lord of hosts; I am the first, and I am the last; and beside me there is no God."*

Isaiah 44:8, *"Fear ye not, neither be afraid: have not I told thee from that time, and have declared it? ye are even my witnesses. Is there a God beside me? yea, there is no God; I know not any."*

John 17:3, *"And this is eternal life, that they might know thee the only true God, and Jesus Christ, whom thou hast sent."*

1 Timothy 2:5, *"For there is one God, and one mediator between God and men, the man Christ Jesus."*

James 2:19, *"Thou believest that there is only one God; thou doest well: the devils also believe and tremble."*[11]

While the foundation of saving Christianity is the Holy Bible, the message of Holy Scripture in Genesis 1:1 does not begin with mankind, but with God! There are many gods (so-called) in the world. Some are carved and fashioned by hand, and others are created by fallible imaginations of human minds. The primary question, then, is *What does the Bible teach?*

---

[11] See also 2 Samuel 7:22; 1 Kings 8:60; Nehemiah 9:6; Psalm 86:10; Isaiah 45:21, 46:9; Romans 3:30; 1 Corinthians 8:4-6; Galatians 3:20; Ephesians 4:6; 1 Timothy 1:17; et al.

The first Christians were dogmatic as to who God is and His nature. Embedded in their spiritual DNA was the belief that He is *not* like humans, but wholly, totally, and altogether different. They understood the LORD's condemnation of ancient Israel during a time of spiritual apostasy: *"...thou thoughtest that I was altogether such a one as thyself"* (Psalm 50:21b). (Through the secularization of universities and institutions of higher learning, the notion that God is nothing more than a higher form of man has poisoned modern culture.) Neither were the first Christians accepting of every entity that was called "God," nor of every religion that said it believed in "God." For them, there was *only* one true and living God. All other gods, so-called, regardless of the sincerity and earnestness of their followers, were human fabrications and satanic counterfeits. Furthermore, there is the misconception entrenched in today's thinking that the God of the Old Testament is not the same as the God of the New Testament; it is wrongly viewed that the God of the OT is one of wrath and anger and the God of the NT is one of love and grace. Nothing could be farther from the truth! The God and Father of our Lord Jesus Christ is the God of Abraham, Isaac, and Jacob (see Matthew 22:32). So, before the message of Christianity can be presented to the point of understanding and belief, you must know about the one and only, true and living, great and immeasurable God of heaven and earth.

## God is the Creator of All Things

`The oft-quoted saying of pagan Roman philosopher Lucretius is absolutely correct: *nothing comes from nothing (ex nihilo nihil fit)*. Even human logic teaches us that things do not magically and suddenly appear out of nowhere. For example, if a paper clip is found in the middle of an open field, you know it did *not* magically appear and cause itself to be placed there. There had to be something before there could be anything! That something or someone is God! God is the First Cause, Intentional Designer, and Creator of all things.[12] A fact that should be noted about the first Christians is this: The more ignorant about God they found an individual, the farther back into the Old Testament they reached to share the gospel. It is no accident, then, that the very first words of the Bible are *"In the beginning God created the heavens and the earth."* Things as they are now did not just "happen," or mystically appear, or slowly evolve over trillions of years. The heavens and the earth — the sun, moon, stars, plants, birds, animals, and everything that exists — were by divine *fiat* (Latin - *let it be done*), an act of design, direct and divine creation. All things were made by Him and for Him, and the time frame was very short — only six normal 24-hour days![13]

A point that must be understood, which will be developed later, is that the crown of all God's creation was man! *"And the Lord God formed man of the dust of the ground, and breathed into his nostrils the breath of life; and man became a living soul."*[14]

This biblical teaching of creation by the direct act of God, *out of nothing,* means that you and the world belong to God, and He is your Sustainer. God is independent of you and the world,

---

[12] Genesis 1:1; Acts 4:24; Colossians 1:16; Revelation 10:6

[13] For further, in-depth study on this subject, see the author's chapter in *A New Exposition of The London Baptist Confession of Faith of 1689*, Rob Ventura, general editor (Christian Focus Publications: Ross-shire, Scotland, 2022) 97-109.

[14] Genesis 2:7

time, and space, but you and the world, time, and space are totally dependent upon Him. Because God made you, you are His possession, and He has rights over you; therefore, you are accountable to Him! This truth of creation is the gateway to all other divine truths.

## God is Spirit

Jesus said, "God is Spirit" (John 4:24). That is, He does *not* have a body of flesh and bones. Jesus did *not* say that God is *a* Spirit; instead, He said that "God **is** Spirit"! Professor J. A. Millikin writes concerning this:

> God is a spiritual Being. The very essence of God's being is Spirit. That is, God has no material element in His essential nature. He does not have a body."[15] As pure Spirit God is invisible (Romans 1:20; 1 Timothy 1:17), and no likeness can be formed of Him (Deuteronomy 4:15-23; Isaiah 40:25), nor can He be apprehended by a physical means (John 4:24; Acts 17:25). Since God is Spirit, He cannot be limited by space, nor can He be confined to any one place (1 Kings 8:27; Acts 7:48-49; 17:24). No one can escape His presence, for He is everywhere (Psalm 139:7-17; Jeremiah 23:23-24). And because God is everywhere, there is nothing you do, whether in secret or in public, in thought, word or deed, good or evil, but what God sees and knows all about it. God knows all things, including the end, even from the beginning.[16]

---

[15] Numbers 23:19; Isaiah 31:3; John 4:24; Luke 24:39

[16] Psalm 139:1-6; Proverbs 15:3; Isaiah 46:10; 1 John 3:20. This quote is taken from *Christian Doctrine for Everyman* (Marion, Arkansas: KRB books, 1976). 24.

# God is Eternal, Infinite, Perfect, Self-sufficient, and Unchanging

But just exactly who is this God who created all things? He is the only Being that is categorically eternal. Job said of Him that the number of His years cannot be searched out (Job 36:26). There has never been a time when God was not God, and He will never cease to exist! As God Himself said to the prophet Isaiah, *"...before me there was no God formed, neither shall there be after me."* and *"...I am the first, and I am the last; and beside me there is no God."* Also, *"...Is there a God beside me yea, there is no God; I know not any."*[17] He is the only one who eternally and infinitely *is*, has always been, and forevermore shall be. As the psalmist David declared, *"Before the mountains were brought forth, or even thou hast formed the earth and the world, even from everlasting to everlasting, thou art God"* (Psalm 90:2). God does not grow old with the passing of time. As it has been said, "There is no wrinkle on the brow of eternity." Every person has a beginning and shall have an earthly end. However, God is the only eternal being, without beginning of days and ending of life.

Furthermore, He is infinite.[18] Immeasurable is the only way to describe Him. There is no way you can measure the greatness or immensity of God! As Solomon prayed at the dedication of the Temple, *"But will God indeed dwell on the earth? Behold, the heaven and heaven of heavens cannot contain Thee; how much less this house that I have builded?"* (1 Kings 8:27). He cannot be calculated or quantified. Nor can He be put into a box. There is no cage large enough to contain Him!

---

[17] Isaiah 43:10; 44:6 & 8
[18] Psalm 90:2; 93:2; Deuteronomy 33:27

Coupled with this is the reality of His absolute perfection. Unlike the pantheon of gods in ancient mythology (Greek, Roman, and Norse), the LORD God is without flaw and does not make mistakes. The God of Christianity is not temperamental; He does not act capriciously or arbitrarily. The LORD is perfect and righteous in in all His ways, and holy in all His works (Psalm 145:17). He did not need to go to school and learn, and He needed no instructor or counselor to educate Him. This is what the prophet Isaiah means when he says, *"With whom took He counsel, and who instructed Him, and taught Him in the path of judgment, and taught Him knowledge, and showed to Him the way of understanding?"* (Romans 11:33-34). As opposed to everyone else, He has never "messed up" or had to learn by trial and error. Jesus states that the Father in heaven is perfect (Matthew 5:48).

Additionally, He is independent of men and women and is completely self-sufficient. The theological term for this reality is *aseity* (Latin – *a se* meaning *from self*). This certifies that the LORD is not dependent upon anyone or anything! Paul the Apostle so powerfully and eloquently declared this truth to the most learned philosophers in ancient Athens (on Mars Hill) when he said, *"Neither is worshipped with men's hands,* **as though he needed anything***, seeing he giveth to all life, and breath, and all things"* (Acts 17:25, **emphasis added**). Simply put, because within Himself God is self-sufficient, He is not lonely and does not need anyone or anything!

Furthermore, He does not change. He is immutable. One thing that is consistent with all of humanity is that we are consistently inconsistent and constantly changing. Not so with God! He is consistently consistent with Himself. People, times, and cultures frequently change, but He does not! He is not like the gods-so-called of Greek and Roman mythology on Mount Olympus or the ones of Norse mythology in Asgard, who were often lecherous, flirtatious, adulterous, deceitful, jealous of one another, scheming and conniving against each other, constantly fluctuating, and changing their minds. The psalmist David proclaims this truth in Psalm 102:25-27. God reveals to the prophet Malachi, *"I am the LORD, I change not; therefore, ye sons of Jacob are not consumed"* (Malachi 3:6). If God changes, then He is not perfect! If He changes it suggests that He either had to correct something from the past or improve upon something for the future. How comforting to know that this perfect God does not vacillate or change with the current flow of feelings, thoughts, and cultures. The apostle James would confirm the same: *"Every good gift and every perfect gift is from above, and cometh down from the Father of lights, with whom there is no variableness, neither shadow of turning"* (James 1:17). You can depend upon Him to be the same through all the varying circumstances of life. He is *not* culturally mutable or changeable, but covenantally faithful to Himself, to all those who believe in Him, and to His eternal purposes. Neither He, nor His truth, ever change. He is the one constant throughout the universe! As the great old hymn, *Immortal, Invisible,* declares it:

> To all life Thou givest, to both great and small.
> In all life Thou livest, the true life of all.
> We blossom and flourish as leaves on the tree,
> And wither and perish but naught changeth Thee.
>
> -Walter C. Smith, 1824-1908-

# God is Ultimately Incomprehensible

What is meant by this expression? It does *not* mean that God cannot be personally and intimately known. He can! As Jesus declared in John 17:3, *"And this is eternal life, that they may know Thee the only true God, and Jesus Christ, whom Thou hast sent."* While a person may really and personally know God, that person cannot know Him fully with ultimate comprehension. Allow me to illustrate. Each believer in Christ knows something of the great power, grace, mercy, and love of God. That was part of Jesus' high-priestly prayer in John 17. Yet, while believers do genuinely know God personally, along with His attributes or perfections, we do **not** know Him perfectly, exhaustively, and with absolute comprehension. Only He knows Himself in this fullness. Furthermore, in heaven the final abode of all true believers, we will continue to learn more and more of all His glory and greatness throughout all eternity. Herein lies a glorious mystery: we know Him, but we will continue to know Him more and more every day (as we reckon time) forever and ever. We will never reach the point where we know Him with absolute perfection. Why? Because God is God, and He will always remain such, and we will always be redeemed sinners saved by His marvelous grace. This barrier and distinction will never be broken down or erased! We will never become God, or equal to Him. Each eternal day we will be filled with increasing wonder and awe at knowing who He is and His unending love for us. Hence, the word *mystery* is used in numerous places in the Holy Bible, and one of those mysteries is the ultimate incomprehensibility of God.

# God is Triune

There are many things in the world and around us which we do not understand and cannot comprehend. Atoms and quarks, and especially oxygen with all its complexities and absolute necessity to everything on the earth prove this point. We should realize there are also a few things about God that we cannot fully understand. Again, this is because God is God, and we cannot comprehend all there is to know about Him. If we could then He would cease to be God and we would be His equal. While it is above our *full* understanding, God's infallible Word, the Holy Bible, clearly teaches that there is only one God;[19] however, there are three Persons making up this God. They are the Father, the Son (Jesus Christ), and the Holy Ghost.[20] Each of them is God – same in substance, equal in essence, position, power, purpose, and glory yet there are *not* three Gods, but only one! Even though this may seem like a contradiction, we must resist using fallible mortal reason and cast ourselves unreservedly upon God's authoritative Word to see what it teaches. A contradiction, no; a mystery, yes!

While the Holy Bible is emphatic that there is **only** one God (see Deuteronomy 6:4), it is equally emphatic that this one true and living God makes Himself known in three Persons: the Father, and the Son, and the Holy Spirit. Again, this does *not* mean that there are three Gods, or that there is one God who functions in three different modes throughout human history (e.g., the Father in the Old Testament, the Son in the New

---

[19] Deuteronomy 6:4; Isaiah 43:10; 44:6 &8; 45:5-6, 21 & 22, 46:9; Mark 12:28-32; 1 Corinthians 8:4; 1 Timothy 2:5; James 2:19.

[20] Matthew 28:19; John 1:1, 2 & 14, 5:18, 20:28; Acts 5:3-4; 1 John 5:7; 2 John 9. I, with studied reason, adhere to the "Johannine Comma" of 1 John 5:7.

Testament, and the Holy Spirit in our present day). This concept of modes is the ancient heresy of Modalism, which was soundly condemned by the Early Church. Instead, the One is Three and the Three are One! The theological term used to describe this biblical truth is the **Trinity**.

There are many verses in the Holy Bible that teach the divine Trinity, beginning with Genesis 1:26 and 11:7 and continuing through the Old Testament into the New Testament. There are the Gospels and their baptismal formula; also, there are the "triadic expressions" in the Epistles of the New Testament (e.g., 2 Corinthians 13:14; 1 Peter 1:2; et al). However, there is one passage that seals the teaching: 1 John 5:7, *"For there are three that bear record in heaven, the Father, the Word [Jesus Christ], and the Holy Ghost: and these three are one."*

One writer has called this truth of the holy Trinity "the ultimate and supreme glory of the Christian faith." Granted, the doctrine of the holy Trinity is a mystery that is impossible to comprehend fully; nevertheless, it is clearly taught in the Holy Bible. As Professor J.I. Packer so clearly states it, "Trinity is the Christian word for describing the Christian God."[21] The Scriptures make it plain that to be an authentic Christian one must believe the Trinity and anyone who does not believe this teaching, is not, nor can be, a true Christian!

---

[21] *Collected Shorter Writings of J.I. Packer*, vol. 1 (Vancouver, British Columbia: Regent College Publishing, 2008) 1. Also, see the writings of the early church Fathers: Tertullian, Athanasius, Chrysostom, Augustine, et al, and study the early church creeds.

# God is All-powerful and Absolutely Sovereign

The unstudied belief today is that God and Satan (the devil) are equal entities engaged in competition on a level playing field. One is good and the other is evil, and the winner is the one to whom a person yields. Nothing could be further from the truth! The Lord God Almighty is the Creator, and Lucifer (i.e., Satan, the devil) is a *created* fallen angel. God alone has *all* power in heaven and in earth. He rules His creation, and all nature, humans, and even Satan, are under His sovereign power and control. Everything that happens is decided by God.[22] Not one single event in all the universe happens by luck or chance.[23] Also, while many things are too hard or impossible with humans, nothing is too hard or impossible for the God of the Bible. As Daniel said, *"And all the inhabitants of the earth are reputed as nothing: and he doeth according to His will in the army of heaven, and among the inhabitants of the earth: and none can stay His hand, or say unto Him, What doest thou?"*[24] Because God is absolutely sovereign, He is *not* bound, controlled, or stymied by nature, the will of man, or the will of Satan!

# God is Everywhere and All-Knowing

The ancient and pagan religions believed there were different gods (or spirits) for different parts of the earth: there

---

[22] Exodus 4:11; Deuteronomy 32:39; Job 1:7-12; Psalm 107:25-29; Proverbs 16:4, 21:1 & 31; Daniel 2:21-22; Amos 3:6; Nahum 1:3-6; Matthew 4:10; Ephesians 1:11.

[23] It is my belief that the word "luck" should be completely eliminated form our vocabulary.

[24] Jeremiah 32:17; Matthew 19:26; Luke 1:37; Daniel 4:35; Psalm 115:3.

were gods of the sea, the mountains and valleys, the forests, even for wind and fire. This was because the deities they conceived in their minds were limited to time and space and could not be everywhere at one time. Not so with the God of the Holy Bible and Christianity. He is everywhere (omnipresent) at the same time; He fills heaven and earth. This truth brings great comfort to the Christian because we know He is always with us.[25]

Furthermore, God is all-knowing (omniscient) and nothing is hidden from Him. He does not have to study, learn, restudy, or reconfigure His plans. He knows perfectly the past, the present, and the future, the things that will and will not be. Nothing can or will take Him by surprise. He knows what you are thinking this very moment and what you will be thinking tomorrow at this hour. His incredible omniscience should comfort us in knowing that He knows everything that comes our way. And it should challenge us to think and always act as if we are always in public, because as it has been said, "For God is always our audience of One." What the most fearful reality to think about is that God knows the hidden secrets of our hearts and Christ will reveal and judge them on the Last Day.[26]

## God is Absolutely Holy and Just

When most people today conceive of God, what is the first thought that comes to mind? Love. Contrary to modern human understanding, the most predominant attribute of God that is found in the Holy Bible is *not* love, but holiness. (The word

---

[25] Psalm 139:7-12; Jeremiah 23:23-24; Acts 17:24-28.
[26] Psalm 139:1-6; Proverbs 15:3; Matthew 6:8, 10:28-29; Hebrews 4:13; 1 John 3:20; Romans 2:16.

"love" is found 310 times in the Bible, and the word "holy," and its cognates, is found 611 times, almost double the number.) Holiness denotes absolute moral purity. It is the one attribute that governs all of God's other perfections. Without His holiness, all His other attributes or perfections would be tainted. His power, justice, grace, love, and mercy would be impure, blemished, imbalanced, and unfair. God's holiness also means He is completely different and separate from all His created beings. He, *alone,* is perfectly pure, good, and righteous in the highest possible sense. *"God is light, and in Him is no darkness at all"* (1 John 1:5). Anything that is evil, and defiles cannot come near unto God, for He is *"of purer eyes than to behold evil, and canst not look on iniquity"* (Habakkuk 1:13).

> The entire Mosaic system of washing; the divisions of the tabernacle;...the insisting upon animal sacrifice as a necessary medium of approach to God; God's directions to Moses in Exodus 3:5, to Joshua in Joshua 5:15; the punishment of Uzziah in 2 Chronicles 26:13-23;...the doom of Korah, Dathan, and Abiram in Numbers 16:1-33; and the destruction of Nadab and Abihu in Leviticus 10:1-3; all these were intended to teach, emphasize, and burn into the minds and hearts of the Israelites the fundamental truth that God is holy, unapproachably holy.[27]

Created angelic beings continuously hover above the throne of God and cry out one to another, day and night, *"Holy, holy,*

---

[27] R.A. Torrey, *What the Bible Teaches; A Thorough and Comprehensive Study of what the Bible has to Say Concerning the Great Doctrines of which it Treats* (Fleming H. Revell Company: London & Edinburgh, 1898) 37.

*holy, Lord God Almighty, which was, and is, and is to come."*[28] It is *not* love, love, love, or grace, grace, grace, or peace, peace, peace, or power, power, power the seraphim continually cry, but **holy, holy, holy!**[29]

Because God is holy, He is just in all His doings. As Abraham says, *"Shall not the Judge of all the earth do right?"* (Genesis 18:25). Yes, He will, and every act He ever performs will be right! His justice demands that He punish all sin and set right all wrongs. Sin and evil cannot be swept under the carpet, but they must be dealt with honestly and fairly. Therefore, God will one day judge the world, *not* according to the fluctuating and vacillating standards of humanity, but in perfect fairness and righteousness.[30]

# God is Merciful and Loving

This is amazing when one thinks of all the other attributes of God. God is merciful and kind, even to those who presently hate him. He does good and shows His love to those who are now His bitterest enemies. *"But God, who is rich in mercy, for his great love wherewith he loved us."* The love of God is from everlasting to everlasting. It is vaster than the Mariana Trench and cannot be fathomed.[31]

Mistakenly, many think that because God is merciful and full of lovingkindness, He will overlook everyone's sins and

---

[28] Isaiah 6:3; Revelation 4:8.
[29] Notice the three-fold repetition of the word "holy." Even here there is the acknowledgment of the triune nature of God.
[30] Isaiah 45:21; John 5:30; Acts 17:31; Revelation 15:3.
[31] Psalm 103:17; Matthew 5:45; John 3:16; Ephesians 2:4.

eventually bring everyone to heaven. Known as *universalism*, this idea is blatantly false! Will the LORD allow the Jack the Rippers, the Adolph Hitlers, and the vilest serial killers and pedophiles of the world into heaven at last? Perish the thought. The sole reason God extends His mercy and goodness and patiently forbears with evil people is to give those who will repent and believe, more time to come to Him for salvation (especially see Acts 17:30-31; Romans 2:4-5).

## Finally, God is Unapproachable

What is meant by *unapproachable*? Are we not commanded in Scripture to come to God? Yes, we are. Nonetheless, there is something behind His invitation to come that must be understood. Unapproachable means that, *in Himself*, God cannot be approached by men and women. Why? Many modern concepts of God are erroneous and lie shallow in the average person's thinking. God is like a spare tire we pull out when we have a flat, or the coin that is put in a parking meter when we find a parking space, or a blank check to give us a miracle and bail us out of trouble, or a magic lantern to rub and get all our desires fulfilled, or a rich, loving old grandpa who we can visit when we need something. For the modern mind, He is anxiously waiting, always readily accessible, and constantly at our disposal. Such are the erroneous concepts of God that many have.

Contrary to these popular and humanistic notions is the biblical revelation of the true and living God. Paul the Apostle declares in 1 Timothy 6:16, *"Who only hath immortality, dwelling in the light which no man can approach unto; whom no man hath seen, nor can see: to whom be honour and power everlasting. Amen."*

It bears repeating, *"dwelling in the light which no man can approach unto."* God dwells in such light that its brilliance would blind us, and He is a consuming fire that His thermal heat would consume us, if we came into His immediate presence unaided or unshielded. Hebrews 12:29 declares: *"For our God is a consuming fire."*

This is never seen more clearly than at the giving of the moral Law – still binding on all people today – at Mt. Sinai. As Moses led the people of Israel to Mt. Sinai, God's manifest presence descended onto the mountain. His presence and holiness were so bright that He covered the mountain with a thick, dark smoke and clouds, caused an alarming trumpet to blast, made the entire mountain quake, and generated thunderings and lightnings to warn the people to not come near but to stand afar off. When the people saw these things, they trembled and were filled with unspeakable fear. Afraid to go near the mountain, they told Moses to speak for them, but not to let *"God speak with us, lest we die."* So, the people stood afar off, and Moses drew near *"unto the darkness where God was."* It was then, out of the thick dark cloud, which shielded him from God's unapproachable brightness, that God gave unto Moses His holy Law, the Ten Commandments.

Not even angelic beings, such as seraphim or cherubim, can look upon God's blinding and dazzling glory (see Isaiah 6:2, cf. Revelation 4:8). These angelic beings have three sets of wings. With one set they hover above God's throne; with another set they cover their feet; and with the third set they cover their faces and eyes. They cannot even look upon the brilliance of His holiness, not even for a nanosecond. The hymnwriter describes well the blinding magnificence and eye-burning luster of the true and living God:

> No angel in the sky
> Can fully bear the sight,
> But downward bends his burning eye
> At mysteries so bright.

-Matthew Bridges, 1851, in *Crown Him with Many Crowns*-

All of the above – the listed attributes or perfections of God – illustrate one crucial and indispensable point that must be understood: God is not like man! He is wholly *other* and completely different from created men and women. This leads to the next consideration, which must be understood.

## What is Man?

Renowned Anglican Bishop J.C. Ryle began his treatise on "What Is Man?" with these words:

> It is the beginning of all true religion to know ourselves. You will never value the Gospel till you know what you are by nature, and what you deserve. I ask you, in all affection, to read carefully what I am going to say about the question – What is man?[32]

And so, I ask you the same. What or who is man? On the sixth day of Creation, perhaps in the middle of the day, the LORD God created the crown of His creation – man. This distinctive being was not an animal. God distinctly created

---

[32] *Home Truths*, vol. 1 (Keyser, West Virginia: Odom Publications, n.d.) 241.

them *male and female!*[33] Unlike all the other creatures, man was created in the image of God, and he had something uniquely and eternally embedded within his being that nothing in the plant or animal kingdom possessed – a living soul (Genesis 2:7). It is the soul that gives humans a God consciousness, which animals do not possess. Animals never worship God. They have no moral conviction against killing other animals, or even humans. They have no problem stealing food from other creatures, and one will never see an animal pause before eating, lift its head, and thank its Creator for its food. Humans do. Why? Because we possess an everlasting and never-dying soul, which informs the mind that there is a God and instructs the conscience of what is right and wrong!

Furthermore, the LORD God created the first human differently than He did the rest of the His creatures. Man was created in "the image of God." What is this image? It, of course, is not the physical image because God does not have a physical body of flesh and bones. It is a spiritual image of righteousness and holiness. This image was passed from Adam to the rest of humanity. All humans possess the image of God within them. However, something took place that would mar and deface (not eradicate) that image, which is seen in the next section.

## Man & the First Sin

God placed the first man and woman, Adam and Eve, in a perfect environment called the Garden of Eden. The Creator commanded them to tend the Garden, to multiply and replenish the earth, subdue it, and have dominion over it

---

[33] In this present-day dysphoric world of gender confusion, there are not 52, or 67, or 72 genders, but only two – male and female (Genesis 1:27)!

(Genesis 1:28). They were free to do anything they desired, except for one thing. They could not eat the fruit of the tree of the knowledge of good and evil. This was their one and only prohibition! God solemnly declared, *"...for in the day that thou eatest thereof thou shalt surely die"* (Genesis 2:15-17).

When Eve *"saw that the fruit was good to eat, pleasant to the eyes, and to be desired to make one wise, she ate of the fruit and then gave some to her husband"* (see Genesis 3:6). This was the first direct act of rebellion by man against God and it was sin; it is *the original sin*. Adam and Eve died that day – not physically, but spiritually (Ephesians 2:1; Romans 5:12 & 18a)! This event is what is known biblically, historically, and theologically as the *Fall*.

After the Fall, did Adam and Eve go rushing to their Creator and ask for His forgiveness? No, Adam and Eve's immediate actions after the Fall demonstrate their spiritual condition. They realized they were naked, ran and hid themselves, and tried to avoid God because they were afraid of truth and what they had done. They grabbed *fig* leaves (lit. Hebrew - *"broad"* leaves) to make garments to cover their nakedness, and sought to clothe themselves, which shows they tried to make themselves presentable to God by the works of their own hands (see Genesis 3:1-10).

When confronted by their Creator, they began to make excuses by shifting the blame of their sinful deeds to each other. Adam blamed Eve and Eve blamed the "serpent" (see Genesis 3:11-13). By this one transgression, Adam and Eve plunged all of humanity into a state of fallenness, sin, and brokenness. Every human being, consequently, inherited this ruinous state from our first father and mother. The results of the Fall concerning humanity are further fleshed out in the rest of Holy Scripture. (This will be developed later.) However, God, in His mercy and love, sought and found Adam and Eve. Immediately, He judged the serpent (Satan), and then Eve, and finally Adam. After pronouncing His judgment upon them, God *killed* an animal, took its skin, and made suitable garments, and properly clothed them. He then drove them from the Garden paradise and sent cherubim (plural) with flaming swords to guard the Garden. This was to keep Adam and Eve from going back in and eating of the Tree of Life, and thus living forever in sin. This narrative is explained in Genesis 3:7-24.

Fast forward to the German philosopher, Friedrich Nietzsche (1844-1900), who believed and taught that man is and can potentially become an *Übermensch* (German word for a *superman*). Since he was an atheist and believed that human reason destroyed any notion of a God, the only thing left to believe in was man (that is, humanity). According to Nietzsche, humans are potentially all-powerful and limitless. A person can be and do anything he wants. I ask, "Oh, really? Can he fly and leap tall buildings with a single bound like Superman? Can he stand on water's edge and with the power of his voice move a hurricane another direction?" There are many things humans are powerless to do. Nonetheless, Nietzsche's philosophies, along with those of Karl Marx, infiltrated the world's universities and have filtered down into today's society. Again, the Holy Bible gives us a different picture of mankind since the Fall of Adam. What is the actual present spiritual condition of all humanity, especially those outside of Christ, who do not know and trust Him as their Lord and Savior?

The common thread of belief running through all humanity is that every person is born innocent and basically good. It is only as the person grows older and sees the bad actions of others that innocence is lost, and the person starts to do wrong and sins. Contrary to that belief, the Holy Bible paints a different picture. God, in the Holy Scriptures, clearly states the truth about men and women in their present condition.[34]

1. All of humanity is spiritually dead. (Did Adam and Eve die on the day they ate of the forbidden fruit? No, and yes. They did *not* die physically, but spiritually!)

Genesis 2:17   *But of the tree of the knowledge of good and evil, thou shall not eat of it; for in the day that thou eatest thereof thou shalt surely die.*

Ephesians 2:1   *And you hath He quickened, who were dead in trespasses and sins.*

2. All of humanity's understanding is darkened.

Ephesians 4:18   *Having the understanding darkened, being alienated from the life of God through the ignorance that is in them, because of the blindness of their heart...*

Romans 3:11   *There is none that understandeth, there is none that seeketh after God.*

**Note**:   Because there is no one who understands his or her true condition, no one seeks after God on his own!

---

[34] Note carefully: Whenever "ye" is seen in the Authorized Version, it refers to "you" in the plural.

3. Man's heart is deceitful and wicked.

Jeremiah 17:9   *The heart is deceitful above all things, and desperately wicked: who can know it?*

4. Man's mind and conscience are defiled.

Titus 1:15   *Unto the pure all things are pure: but unto them that are defiled and unbelieving is nothing pure; but even their mind and conscience is defiled.*

5. Man is without spiritual strength.

Romans 5:6   *For when we were yet without strength, in due time Christ died for the ungodly.*

6. Man is without righteousness.

Romans 3:10   *As it is written, There is none righteous, no, not one:*

7. Man cannot spiritually hear and understand the Word of God.

John 8:43   *Why do ye not understand My speech? even because ye cannot hear My word.* (**NOTE**: Jesus' audiences heard him physically but did not hear Him spiritually.)

8. Man cannot receive the Holy Spirit.

John 14:17a   *Even the Spirit of truth; whom the world cannot receive. . .*

9. Man cannot understand the Word of God.

<u>1 Corinthians 2:14</u>   *But the natural man receiveth not the things of the Spirit of God: for they are foolishness unto him: neither can he know them, because they are spiritually discerned.*

10.   Man is blinded and controlled by Satan.

<u>2 Corinthians 4:4</u>   *In whom the god of this world hath blinded the minds of them who believe not, lest the light of the glorious gospel of Christ, who is the image of God, should shine unto them.*

<u>2 Timothy 2:24-26</u>   *And the servant of the Lord must not quarrel; but be gentle unto all men, apt to teach, patient, in meekness correcting those that oppose themselves; if God peradventure will give them repentance to the acknowledging of the truth, and that they may recover themselves [come to their senses and escape] out of the snare of the devil, who are taken captive by him at his will.*

11.   Man is not able or willing to come to God by his own strength, power, or freewill; nor can he prepare himself to come to Christ or aid in his own salvation.

<u>Isaiah 64:7a</u>   *And there is none that calleth upon Thy name, that stirreth up himself to take hold of Thee:*

<u>Jeremiah 10:23</u>   *O Lord, I know that the way of man is not in himself; it is not in man that walketh to direct his steps.*

<u>Jeremiah 13:23</u>   *Can the Ethiopian change his skin, or the leopard his spots? then may ye also do good, that are accustomed to doing evil.*

<u>Matthew 23:37</u>   *O Jerusalem, Jerusalem, thou that killest the prophets, and stonest them which were sent unto thee, how often would I have gathered thy children together, even as a hen gathereth her chickens under her wings, and ye would not!*

John 5:40   *And ye will not come to Me, that ye might have life.*

John 1:12-13   *But as many as received him, to them gave He power to become the sons of God, even to them that believe on his name; who were born, not of blood, nor of the will of the flesh,* **nor of the will of man,** *but of God.* (**Emphasis added**)

John 6:44   *No man can come to Me, except the Father which hath sent Me draw him: and I will raise him up at the last day.*

Romans 9:16   *So then it is not him who willeth, nor of him that runneth, but of God that showeth mercy.*

Romans 7:18   *For I know that in me (that is, in my flesh,) dwelleth no good thing: for to will is present with me; but how to perform that which is good I find not.*

**Note**: Paul wrote these words almost 20 years after being converted (that is, saved) on the road to Damascus. He acknowledged that he did not have power or ability even in his Christian life to do what he should do. If a saved person does not have the power, how much less does a lost person? In 1 Corinthians 7:25, Paul said he *". . . obtained mercy of the Lord to be faithful,"* and Jesus said in John 15:5, *". . .for without Me you can do nothing."* Also, in John 3:27, Jesus said, *"A man can receive nothing unless it be given to him from heaven."*

12. Man is a total sinner in every aspect of his being, including his will.

<u>Romans 3:23</u>   *For all have sinned, and come short of the glory of God.*

No better summary of the spiritual state of mankind can be found anywhere, in all writings sacred and secular, than in *The Epistle of Paul to the Romans;* his longest and most thorough epistle. Turn to chapter three and read verses 9-18. This concluding paragraph is a sobering illustration, and it as if the Apostle is standing over an open spiritual grave and looking down into it. Like a coroner, who examines a physical body, the apostle Paul opens with a general spiritual description and then outlines a specific examination of each part from head to toe, as if he is looking at a corpse in a grave. What is Paul's conclusion? *There is death down there!*

Here, then, is the present-state of all humanity, regardless of where in the world a person may dwell. He or she is fallen in Adam, spiritually dead in trespasses and sin, a sinner by birth, nature, and choice; totally depraved in soul and body; and the spiritual image of God is marred and severely damaged.[35] No one can correctly understand and discern the true things of God without the divine assistance of the Holy Spirit. Furthermore, everyone is inherently self-righteous, a breaker of the Law of God, a spurner of the gospel of the grace of God, broken, and without authentic hope apart from Jesus Christ. These truths are the divinely revealed declarations of the Holy Bible and are expressed in various Christian confessions of faith. For example:

> Our first parents [Adam and Eve], by this sin, fell from their original righteousness and communion with God,

---

[35] This is theologically called "the Noetic Effects of the Fall." The word *"noetic"* comes from the Greek word *"nous,"* which means "mind."

and *we in them*, whereby death came upon all: all becoming dead in sin, and wholly defiled in *all* the faculties and parts of soul and body.[36]

## What is Sin?

People are so prone to talk of mistakes and "mess-ups." The words *transgressions, iniquities,* and *sin* are almost extinct from present-day vocabularies, especially the word *sin*. Nevertheless, sin still exists. What is it? At Creation, God wrote His law upon Adam's mind and heart, along with *all* Adam's posterity (Romans 2:15). It was later codified and written on tablets of stone at Mount Sinai and is called the Ten Commandments. It taught Adam, Israel, the Early Church, and now us today how to love God and live for Him in a corrupt world. Contrary to popular thinking, God's law is very *"holy and just, and good"* (Romans 7:12). It can be summed up like this:

I. Thou shalt have no other gods before Me.
II. Thou shalt not make unto thee any graven image.
III. Thou shalt not take the name of the Lord thy God in vain.
IV. Remember the Sabbath day, to keep it holy. (See the entirety of the commandment in Exodus 20:8-11.)
V. Honor thy father and thy mother.
VI. Thou shalt not kill.
VII. Thou shalt not commit adultery.
VIII. Thou shalt not steal.

---

[36] *The London Baptist Confession of Faith of 1689*, chapter 6, paragraph 2. Emphasis added. "All the faculties" includes the will, which, too, is in bondage to sin. See Martin Luther's classic *The Bondage of the Will*.

IX. Thou shalt not bear false witness against thy neighbor.
X. Thou shalt not covet.[37]

Sin, then, is a breaking of this law! Furthermore, if a person breaks *one* of these, he or she is guilty of breaking them *all* (cf. 1 John 3:4; Galatians 3:10-12; Romans 3:20)! The law is a chain. If one link is broken, the apostle James declares that the entire chain is broken (see James 2:10-11). Jesus interpreted the law more strictly in the New Testament and said that the two great principles on which the law is built are these: "Thou shalt love the Lord thy God with all thy heart, and with all thy soul, and with all thy strength, and with all thy mind; and thy neighbor as thyself" (Matthew 5:21-32; Luke 10:27; Mark 12:30-31).

## Sin and You!

As you read the Ten Commandments, if you are totally honest with yourself, you are made keenly aware that you have broken at least one, if not several of them. And added to the seriousness of this, you will have to admit that you have broken several of these commandants *willfully*. You are a transgressor of God's law; again, a sinner by birth, nature, practice, and choice![38] Your sins have separated you from God and you lack the power and ability to change or remedy your condition![39] Many sincere people know they have not done right and seek to "turn over a new leaf" in their lives. Oftentimes, "New Year's resolutions" quickly evaporate. Soon people are back into the

---

[37] Exodus 20:1-17; Deuteronomy 5:6-22.
[38] Psalm 51:5; Isaiah 64:6; Romans 3:9-19 & 23; Ephesians 2:2-3.
[39] Isaiah 64:7; Jeremiah 10:23, 13:23; John 1:12-13; Romans 7:18.

same patterns and are no better off, either before God or within themselves. This is the power of sin!

The Word of God makes it plain that God is angry with the wicked every day. It declares "the soul that sins shall surely die," and "the wages of sin is death."[40] Romans 1:18 declares that God's wrath is "revealed from heaven against all ungodliness and unrighteousness of men," and unless His anger can be turned away before you die, you will be sent to the lake of fire and brimstone where you will experience the unmitigated fury of God forever and ever. This is called *the second death!*[41] As you read this you may think, *If all the above is true, is there a way of escape?* This is a good question, and the simple answer is a positive YES! The full answer is found in the good news of the gospel outlined below.

## Jesus Christ, His Person

"He [Jesus] is a constant challenge to men, to the greatest of men. It was so at the first, and it is true today," wrote renown New Testament Greek scholar, A.T. Robertson.[42] Who, then, in the world is Jesus Christ and what in the world did He come to do? The Bible teaches us exactly about Him. More than just another famous figure in human history, He is eternal. Like the description of Melchizedek, the ancient priest in Abraham's day, He eternally is *"without father, without mother, without descent, having neither beginning of days, nor end of life"* (see Genesis 14:18; Psalm 110:4; Hebrews 5:3 & 10, 6:20, 7:3). Jesus was **not** the first thing God created, and He did not come into

---

[40] Genesis 2:17; Ezekiel 18:20; Romans 6:23.
[41] John 3:36; Matthew 25:31-46; Revelation 20:11-15; 21:8.
[42] *Epochs In The Life Of Jesus*, (New York: Charles Scribner's Son, 1947) 1-2.

existence with His conception in the womb and birth of the virgin Mary in Bethlehem of Judea. He is before all time and is the eternally existent *Word* (Gk. *logos)*, the eternal second Person of the holy Trinity. He existed even before the "beginning," as we know it. As John, the beloved Apostle, emphatically states, *"In the beginning was the Word, and the Word was with God, and the Word was God"* (John 1:1). This same John closes out the canon of Holy Scripture, the Book of Revelation, with Jesus' description of Himself – *"I am Alpha and Omega, the first and the last, the beginning and the end"* (Revelation 22:13).

Because God is unapproachable and man is in the state of sinfulness and utter helplessness, God, in His grace and mercy, did something wonderful and unspeakably glorious: He became man and revealed Himself in flesh and blood! The eternal Son, the second Person of the holy Trinity, was conceived by the Holy Ghost in Mary's virgin womb, contrary to the laws of nature without the instrumentality of a man and was born in the town of Bethlehem. He became a man of flesh and blood, possessing a reasonable mind and soul: Immanuel, God with us. He did not cease being what He had always been – God – but He became something He was not before – man. Thus, Jesus became the God-man![43] "His life did not begin when He was born, nor did it end when He died."[44]

He lived most of His life as a carpenter in the obscure village of Nazareth. While He dwelt among men and lived like them, He was different from men in that He was *not* a sinner. Jesus

---

[43] Gk. – *theanthropos*. Matthew 1:18-25; John 1:1-14; 1 Timothy 3:16.
[44] A.T. Robertson, *Epochs In The Life Of Jesus*, 5.

could not and did not sin, but kept the law of God perfectly, in every minute detail.[45]

When He was approximately thirty years old – three years before His crucifixion in Jerusalem – Jesus began His public ministry. He went about preaching and teaching, performing many miracles, and doing good. In His preaching, Jesus constantly called men and women from their empty religions and vain pursuits to a living and personal faith in Himself. He would say things such as, *"Come unto me, all ye that labour [are weary] and are heavy laden, and I will give you rest"* (Matthew 11:28). Also, *"If any man thirst, let him come to me, and drink. He that believeth on Me, as the Scripture hath said, out of his belly shall flow rivers of living water"* (John 737b-28). Why was He doing this? Because God, in His foreordained purpose, planned to save people, to rescue and deliver them from their sin and its awful consequence through Jesus, the perfect Substitute.[46]

## Jesus Christ, His Work – the Cross

Jesus did *not* come to be a great teacher or a compassionate social worker or an equalizer of social injustice. While Jesus performed many miracles, did mighty deeds, and righted many wrongs, this was *not* His primary purpose in coming into the world. As we have seen, you have sinned and your sins have separated you from God, who is thrice holy. Every sin must be paid for and punished.

God has ordained one of two parties to pay the penalty of sin — either you or Christ. Also, He has appointed two places

---

[45] Hebrews 4:14; 7:26; 1 Peter 2:22.
[46] Acts 2:22; John 8:23-24; Matthew 1:21.

where sin is dealt with. The first is the lake of fire, where people suffer eternally as punishment for their own unrepented and unforgiven sins. The second is the Cross, where the God-man, Jesus Christ, suffered and died as a divine Substitute for the sins of others. The Cross was the God-appointed place where the believer's sin was not only dealt with, but actually taken away.[47]

This is why the gospel, which means good news, is so blessed! Since death and the shedding of blood (demonstrated by the Old Testament animal sacrifices) was the only thing that could atone and pay for sin, Jesus came as the Lamb of God to die on the Cross and shed His blood for sins which were not His own. As a result of Christ's dying and taking away sins, He turned away God's divine wrath from others and absorbed it Himself, which is *propitiation*. This successfully brought about reconciliation.[48]

Now sinners, just like yourself, can be brought from a state of separation, condemnation, and alienation into a saving union and vital relationship with God, known as *reconciliation*. *"For Christ also hath once suffered for sins, the just for the unjust, that He might bring us to God, being put to death in the flesh."*[49] Thus, Jesus became the **only** mediator between God and mankind (1 Timothy 2:5)! This is truly good news!

Jesus, as the Lamb of God and God-appointed Substitute, did *not* take away the sins and turn away God's wrath for everyone. He only took away the sins of all those in every age who repent

---

[47] Ephesians 2:16; Colossians 2:13-14; 1 Peter 2:24.

[48] Isaiah 53:5; 10-12; Romans 3:25; 1 Corinthians 5:3; Galatians 1:4; Titus 2:14; Hebrews 1:3; 9:26-28; 10:12; 1 John 4:10.

[49] Romans 5:10; 2 Corinthians 5:18; Hebrews 2:17; 1 Peter 3:18.

and believe in Him. *"...and he that believeth not the Son shall not see life; but the wrath of God abideth on him"* (John 3:36). Polycarp was a direct disciple of the apostle John and early church Father and martyr. He correctly interprets John 1:29 and explains that Jesus as the Lamb of God *"suffered for the salvation of the whole world of those that are saved."*[50]

## Jesus Christ, His Resurrection and Ascension

Even though Jesus died on the cross, three days later He was bodily resurrected from the grave. This was the Father's way of showing His satisfaction with Christ's work on the cross. Furthermore, it is the proof that Jesus is not only a man but the second Person of the Godhead (i.e., Romans 1:4) and it is proof that God has appointed a future day of judgement for all people (Acts 17:30-31). After showing Himself to His disciples, who thought they had seen a spirit, Jesus said, *"Behold my hands and my feet, that it is I myself: handle me, and see; for a spirit hath not flesh and bones, as ye see me have."* Christ then showed Himself alive by *"many infallible proofs,"* especially to *"above five hundred brethren at once."*[51]

Forty days after His resurrection, Jesus ascended back into heaven. He ascended from the Mount of Olives in the presence of His disciples and sat down at the Father's right hand. There

---

[50] Eusebius Pamphilus of Caesarea (c. 265-339), quoted in *Eusebius' Ecclesiastical History*: Complete and Unabridged, translated by Arthur Cushman McGiffert (Pantianos Classics: 1890) 76. Some have wrongly interpreted this verse to teach that everyone will be saved. The "world" here refers to the world of believers, who are or will be saved.

[51] Matthew 28:6; Luke 24:39; Acts 1:3; Romans 4:25; 1 Peter 1:21; cf. 1 Corinthians 15:5-8.

He remains – alive – as the only Mediator between God and man: the *only* Way, the *only* Truth, and the *only* Life.[52]

# The Offices of Jesus Christ

Presently sitting at the Father's right hand as the *only* Mediator between God and man, Christ is quite active in the affairs of this world. To carry on His mediatorial work, He holds three divine offices. One of the offices He fulfills is that of a Prophet. As Prophet, Christ teaches sinners their need for salvation, and Christians are taught how to worship, live, and daily walk in fellowship with their God. He teaches outwardly by the Word of God – the Bible – and inwardly by His Spirit. Since Christ was the last Prophet and is alive and active in heaven, there is no need for prophets today.[53]

Another office that Christ fulfills is that of Priest. While on the earth, Jesus filled the office of Priest by offering Himself *once* as a sacrifice for sin.[54] Now in heaven, He is continually applying His sacrificial work on the cross to the Father, as the sufficient basis for bestowing His pardoning grace and salvation to believing sinners. Because of Christ's priestly intercession for believers, they shall be kept from falling, shall persevere, and shall enter heaven at last. There is no need for priests or priesthoods today because Christ "ever liveth" and is the last and eternal High Priest.[55]

---

[52] Acts 1:11; 1 Timothy 2:5; 3:16; John 14:6.
[53] Deuteronomy 18:15; Matthew 21:33-46 (esp. v. 37); John 7:40; Acts 3:22-26; Hebrews 1:1-2.
[54] Hebrews 7:26-27; 9:14; Revelation 1:5.
[55] John 17:20; Hebrews 8:1-6; 1 Peter 1:5; Hebrews 3:1; 7:21-25.

The last office that Christ fulfills in heaven as Mediator is that of King. The early Christians were constantly preaching that there is *"another King, one Jesus."*[56] When He sat down at the Father's right hand, *all* things were put under His feet and He became the head over *all* things (Ephesians 1:20-23). The Word of God makes it clear that Christ is ruling and reigning from heaven now, even though it may not appear to be so! And while the world looks to be a mess, and the truth of Christ as King is doubted, there shall be a day when He shall return to establish fully His kingdom and prove that He alone is King of kings and Lord of lords.[57] Hallelujah!

## Becoming a Christian

I hope at this point in reading that you believe there is a God, who exists. If so, good, but it is not good enough! The apostle James reminds us, *"Thou believest that there is one God; thou doest well: the devils also believe, and tremble"* (James 2:19). More is needed than simple belief that there is a God. Now, we come to some pivotal questions. Maybe you are asking them already. *How does all this apply to me? How do I become a Christian? How can I be saved and have the forgiveness of my sins? I am basically good; do I really need a Savior? Am I too sinful, will God accept me? Are there any ordinances or rituals that I must perform before I am saved? Do I have to have a special feeling before I become a Christian? Must I clean up my act and become good before becoming a Christian?* These are all good questions (from different perspectives) that deserve biblical answers.

---

[56] Acts 17:6-7.
[57] Ephesians 1:20-23; 1 Corinthians 15:24-28; 1 Timothy 6:15; 1 Peter 3:22; Revelation 1:5; 17:14 & 19:15-16.

Before I answer these questions, let me tell you something that is generally true of almost every person in the world: people are essentially moralists (that is, they unconsciously hold to moralism). What do I mean by moralism? Simply put, most individuals try to be good people, try to do good things, and try to live a good life. They think and hope that being "good" will cause them to be accepted into heaven when they die. They are banking on their personal moral goodness. All of this supposed goodness is bypassing the substitutionary and sacrificial death of Christ on the cross for sin! (**Note carefully**, that *if* you could do *one* good thing that would earn God's acceptance, then Jesus needed not to come, live, die, and rise again.) Some questions must be considered: *If being "good" is all that is required by God, why did Jesus Christ die on the cross? How much goodness is required? Is 25%, 50%, 75%, or even 95% acceptable and good enough to get me into heaven?* No, my friend, you need someone "gooder" than yourself to enter heaven *safely!* (I know "gooder" is not a correct English word, but it is an excellent theological one.) If moralism is ***not*** good enough, what then is needed?

Jesus gave the answer to Nicodemus (one of the most religious persons in all ancient Israel): "You must be born again." Let it be established from the outset that the new birth and conversion to Christ are ***not*** temporary psychological and emotional anomalies, but authentic lasting experiences. They come about neither by physical birth nor by human endeavor, but by a divine operation of grace generated by the Holy Spirit, the third Person of the Godhead. Regeneration (being reborn) is a life-giving miracle of God upon the soul of one who is spiritually dead in trespasses and sin (Ephesians 2:1-10; Titus 3:3-5). It restores the marred, severely damaged, and broken image of God in the soul. A person must be brought from spiritual death to life, from spiritual blindness to spiritual sight, and have a heart of stone replaced with a heart of flesh. Only Jesus Christ by the power of the Holy Spirit can do this!

## Counting the Cost

The door of salvation stands wide open to all who will enter in. There is no individual too hard for Christ to save and none so bad that He will not receive them. You cannot buy salvation and the forgiveness of sins, and there are no special feelings you must experience or ordinances you must perform before you are saved. Salvation comes as a free gift of God's grace! Salvation is of the Lord.[58]

While salvation is free, it is not cheap! There is a cost involved in being a Christian. If you become a Christian, it means that Christ from this day on must rule your life. You will give up things that that you have done all your life and do other things that you have never before done. People may think you are fanatical or have "gone crazy." Friends and perhaps family members may oppose you and even become your enemies. The humanistic philosophies of the world, which have always hated Christ and orthodox Christianity, will bitterly oppose you in society. Jesus said, *"If the world hates you, you know that it hated Me before it hated you"* (John 15:18). Some of this is very hard to hear and bear, but the joy of sins forgiven, possessing a meaningful life, and the assurance of everlasting life far outweigh the costs. Jesus said, *"And whosoever doth not bear his cross, and come after me, cannot be my disciple."*[59] In becoming a

---

[58] Jonah 2:9; Romans 6:23; Ephesians 2:8-9; Philippians 2:13; Titus 3:5.
[59] Luke 14:25-33.

Christian, you must repent of your sins, trust Jesus Christ alone to save you, and follow Him all the days of your life.

## Repentance from Sin

Repentance is a change of mind that is accomplished by godly sorrow for sins and is evidenced by turning around and completely forsaking them. To repent, you must turn from anything you know to be sin and contrary to God's Word and turn to God.[60]

While repentance is something you must do or you will perish, you cannot repent in your own strength. To completely break with sin and its reigning power is beyond human capability. God must grant you the grace and enable you to repent. Repentance is a gift of God.[61]

## Faith in Christ

Faith in Christ consists of three things. The first element is *knowledge*. You must *know* that *"Christ Jesus came into the world to save sinners."* The Son of Man, the Lord Jesus Christ, entered the world *"to seek and to save that which was lost."* He died upon the cross to *"save His people from their sins."* As Prophet, Priest, and King, He is the **only** Mediator between God and man. He, by Himself *alone,* has the power to save you.[62]

The second element of faith in Christ is *belief.* You must not only know these facts about Christ, His Person, and work,

---

[60] Ezekiel 14:6: 18:23; Acts 26:20; 2 Corinthians 7:10-11; 1 Thessalonians 1:9.
[61] Luke 13:3 & 5; Acts 3:26, 5:31, 11:18; 2 Timothy 2:25-26.
[62] 1 Timothy 1:15; Matthew 1:21; 1 Timothy 2:5; Luke 19:10.

especially His resurrection from the dead, but *believe* from the mind and heart that these are true, and that He *can* and *will* save you.

The third element of faith in Christ is *trust*. Christ is the only person who is called the Savior! Believing Christ to be the ***only*** One with the power and ability to save, you must cast yourself upon Him and *trust* Him to do the impossible, to save you and put you in a right relationship with God. To trust someone else for salvation, rather than relying upon yourself, is a difficult demand. This concept is totally foreign to the natural human mind and reasoning, yet it is the truth of God. The reason why you may find this hard to receive is because you have a sinfully proud and stubborn nature. The Lord Jesus Himself must give you the faith to believe.[63] Faith in Jesus Christ is a saving grace which you receive and whereby you rest upon Him *alone* for salvation.

## Justification

When an individual realizes that he is a sinner and comes to Christ in true repentance and faith, God not only saves him, but also justifies him. To be justified means to be declared righteous. God pronounces, accepts, and treats the believing sinner as though he himself had personally obeyed and suffered all that Jesus obeyed and suffered. In other words, a divine transaction or exchange occurs when there is faith in the all-sufficient work of Christ on the cross. God dealt with Jesus on the cross on account of what sinners justly deserve (i.e., He bore God's wrath for sin), and He deals with believing sinners now

---

[63] Acts 3:16; Philippians 1:29; Hebrews 12:2; 2 Peter 1:1.

on account of what Jesus deserves (i.e., they receive His righteousness and justification).[64] As the apostle Paul says, *"For He hath made Him to be sin for us, who knew no sin; that we might be made the righteousness of God in Him"* (2 Corinthians 5:21). In other words, God takes away the person's sins and *imputes,* or puts to the account of that person, the perfect righteousness of Jesus Christ. This is the only righteousness that will allow anyone to enter *safely* into God's holy presence in heaven at last.

Let me ask you, When you stand before God at the last day, whose righteousness would you rather have? Your own, which is sinful, imperfect, flawed, and as "filthy rags" (Isaiah 64:6), or Christ's, which is perfect in every way? The desire of the blessed Apostle was to *"be found in Him (Christ), not having mine own righteousness, …but that which is through the faith of Christ, the righteousness which is of God by faith."*[65] Justification will give you that untainted righteousness and set you free from the bondage of self-righteousness and your own flawed, imperfect works! Furthermore, it will give you Christ's impeccable righteousness, which will grant you *safe* entrance into God Almighty's holy presence.

## A Great Certainty

Christianity is truly unique in its view of life after death. Death on earth does *not* end it all. Some religions, especially those in the Far East, hold to reincarnation: the belief that upon death, the soul is reincarnated into another form on earth, until a state of perfect enlightenment is achieved, and the soul finally goes into nirvana, or some other state of bliss. Animists, those

---

[64] Romans 3:23-26, 4:23-25; Galatians 3:24.
[65] Romans 3:19-28; 5:1; 10:1-4; Galatians 2:16; Philippians 3:9.

who believe in all sorts of spirit beings, including ancestral worship, think that at death each person becomes a spirit and joins the celestial Spirits (or ancestors) in the sky. Many native Americans and primitive tribal groups embrace this belief. Others are nihilists, who believe there is no life after death. Upon death, they believe, the body and soul simply cease to exist: there is no afterlife.

The Holy Bible, however, reveals something totally different. There is life after death for everyone. All souls will be resurrected from the dead on the Last Day of human history when Christ returns in the brightness of His second coming. The human soul is immortal and will exist somewhere for all eternity. Eventually, you will die and one day stand before God at the Judgment. Death seals your destiny. There will *not* be any second chances after death because the Word of God plainly states, *"And as it is appointed unto men once to die, but after this the judgment."*[66]

Furthermore, the Holy Bible is very explicit about who will do the judging. It is not merely God, but Jesus Christ, specifically. The One, whom the world despised and rejected, will be the One by whom all peoples will be judged. There are two distinct verses, among many, which confirm this point:

Acts 17:31 – *"Because He hath appointed a day, in the which He will judge the world in righteousness by that man whom He hath ordained; whereof He hath given assurance unto all men, in that He hath raised Him [Jesus] from the dead."*

---

[66] Ecclesiastes 11:3; Revelation 22:11; Hebrews 9:27; Acts 17:31.

Romans 2:16 – *"In the day when God shall judge the secrets of men by Jesus Christ according to my gospel."*

Romans 2:16 notes that it is not just the works that people do but the "secrets" of their minds and hearts that will be revealed and judged! This is, indeed, a sobering thought. On that great Judgment Day, there will be *no* grading curve or social promotion!

When carefully studied, the Scriptures make clear that there are *only* two places where your human soul and body will dwell after the resurrection. There are no such states as "limbo" or "purgatory" after death. If you do not receive Christ and His perfect righteousness, you will be sent to the "lake which burneth with fire and brimstone" forever and ever. But if you trust Christ as your Savior and Lord, you will enter the rich and glorious joys of heaven forever.[67] Which will it be for you? You may think, *I do not believe this folklore. This is all Western cultural nonsense. This is the twenty-first century, and people are too educated and enlightened to embrace the superstitions of a bygone era.* But let me remind you – **your unbelief does not negate the existence of these divine realities!**

# Calling Upon God

Your unavoidable responsibility at this moment is to call upon God. Being saved is a divine transaction between you and Him. Is there little or no meaning in your life? Does life seem empty? Have you messed up your life in many ways that cannot be repaired? Are you loaded with guilt? Or, are you "successful"

---

[67] Revelation 20:10-22:5. There are too many verses proving these points to list them in this footnote.

and filled with life's pleasures and treasures, yet not satisfied? Are you tired of your sin, and do you want to do away with it ruling your life? Do you feel empty and alone? Do you want to be saved from the judgment to come and know the present joy of sins forgiven? Do you desire a personal and living relationship with God, through Jesus Christ as your Saviour, Lord, and Friend? Do you want a new life that is abundant and full of meaning? Will you right now call upon God, in the name of Jesus Christ, and ask Him to do this wondrous work of salvation in your mind, heart, and life?

You might say, "I don't know how to pray." God is not interested in flowery words and elegant speeches. He will hear anyone who sincerely prays to Him from a humble heart. When you pray to God you should do the following:

- Acknowledge and confess your sins.
- Acknowledge that you deserve to be eternally punished for your sins.
- Confess that you have no power to save yourself.
- Ask the Lord Jesus to help you repent and believe.
- Ask Him to save you and be the Lord of your life.
- Finally, trust God to hear and do according to His promises in the Bible (that is, *"Whosoever shall call upon the name of the Lord shall be saved."*[68] and *"Believe on the Lord Jesus Christ, and thou shalt be saved, and thy house"*) [69]

Jesus spoke of a man praying for salvation: *"...and the publican standing afar off, would not lift up so much as his eyes unto*

---

[68] Romans 10:9-13; Isaiah 55:6-7.
[69] Acts 16:31.

*heaven, but smote upon his breast, saying God be merciful to me a sinner. I tell you, this man went down to his house justified rather that the other: for every one that exalteth himself shall be abased; and he that humbelth himself shall be exalted."*[70]

## What's Next?

After conversion there are three important things you should do. *First,* if you do not have a copy of the Holy Bible, you must get one and begin to read it. The Bible is the most unique book in the world. It is not like an internet blog or a classic novel. It was divinely and inerrantly inspired by God, is the *only* source of Christian faith and practice, and has been preserved unto this very day. God will speak to you as you read and reread it![71] You could begin by reading the fourth book in the New Testament, *The Gospel according to John.*[72]

*Second,* you should immediately seek to find a Bible-focused and Christ-centered church. There you will worship, be taught from the Holy Scriptures, meet Christian friends, have encouraging fellowship, and begin the long and joyous process of growing in grace.[73] You will recognize a biblical and historical New Testament church because it will proclaim and expound the truths found in this book. If you cannot find such a church,

---

[70] Luke 18:9-14.
[71] *May I Introduce You to The Holy Bible?* Earl M. Blackburn (Elkin, North Carolina: Veritas Heritage Press, 2021, www.veritasheritagepress.com).
[72] John 20:31; cf. 2 Timothy 3:16.
[73] Hebrews 10:25; 2 Peter 3:18.

contact the address listed on the last page, or get in touch with the person who gave you this small book.[74]

Third, you should be baptized in water. This is a command of the Lord Jesus Christ and is not optional.[75] It is an outward physical testimony of an inward spiritual reality. Baptism is an illustration of a divine reality: Christ died for your sins, was buried, and raised to life. Similarly, when you go under the water, you are confessing that you have died to your sins, your sins are buried, and you have been raised to walk in newness of life. Baptism does not make you more saved, nor does it take away any sins – only the blood of Christ can do that. Rather, it is an outward confession of Christ and *"the answer a good conscience toward God"* (1 Peter 3:21).

Confusion exists among much of Christendom today regarding baptism. Many think this watery act makes them a Christian or saves them. It does neither. Let me reiterate what is said above. The purpose of baptism is to show our identification with Christ. Just as He died for our sins, was buried, and rose again the third day, so we, by our baptism, declare that when we were saved, we died to our sins and sinful past, our sins were buried or carried away, and we were raised to walk in newness of life.[76] Baptism is, then, an outward demonstration and confession to the world (and the church)

---

[74] See also *Jesus Loves the Church and So Should You,* Earl M. Blackburn (Birmingham, Alabama: Solid Ground Christian Books, 2010).

[75] Matthew 28:18-20; Mark 16:15-16. See also *May I Introduce You to Christian Baptism?* (Elkin, North Carolina: Veritas Heritage Press, 2022, www.veritasheritagepress.com).

[76] Romans 6:3-5.

that you are a disciple and follower of the blessed Lord Jesus Christ.

In conclusion, there is one final point to consider. The moments following the revelation to Peter that Jesus is the Christ, the Son of the living God, Jesus asks two questions and makes a striking remark. These should capture your undivided attention and be your lingering thoughts after reading this treatise. Jesus first asks, *"For what shall it profit a man, if he shall gain the whole word, and lose his own soul?"* And He then asks, *"Or what shall a man give in exchange for his soul?"* Searching questions, indeed!

These questions are followed by a compelling declaration, *"Whosoever therefore shall be ashamed of me and of my words in this adulterous and sinful generation; of him also shall the Son of man be ashamed, when he cometh in the glory of his Father with the holy angels."* Here is the promise of God: If you are ashamed of Christ and deny Him before others, He will be ashamed of you and deny you before the Father. Conversely, if you confess Christ Jesus before men, He will confess you before the Father on the Last Day.[77] Which will it be for you?

This, then, is a humble attempt to present the basic message of biblical, apostolic, and orthodox Christianity, minus the various denominational trappings. Also, consider that there are many more wonderful truths of Christianity that have not been included in this treatise, yet are wonderfully rich and soul-stirring. You have now taken the time to read this small book of Christianity's foundational message, and for that I commend you. Will you not do the same as Luke, the writer of the third

---

[77] Mark 8:34-38; Matthew 10:32.

Gospel in the New Testament, and thoroughly investigate and contemplate this message? If so, upon discovering and embracing its original fullness, you will have peace that passes understanding and eternal life now and forevermore. May the Lord God Almighty grant you the grace to do so. Then one day, Jesus will present you faultless before the presence of His glory with exceeding joy.[78] Amen.

---

[78] Jude 24.

## The Doxology

Praise God from whom all blessings flow,
Praise Him all creatures here below.
Praise Him above ye heavenly host:
Praise Father, Son, and Holy Ghost. Amen!

## The Gloria Patri

Glory be to the Father
and to the Son and to the Holy Ghost,
as it was in the beginning,
is now and ever shall be,
world without end. Amen, amen!

# VERITAS HERITAGE PRESS

*Veritas* is Latin meaning *truth*. Veritas Heritage Press (VHP) is a publishing entity established for the purpose of proclaiming truth and leaving a legacy of truth for the generations to come. This is to be done by publishing and distributing truth – not the subjective ideas and philosophical reasoning of fluctuating cultures, but the divinely revealed, objective, and unchanging truth of the Holy Scriptures: the inspired, inerrant, infallible, authoritative, clear, preserved, and sufficient Word of God, the 66 books of the Holy Bible.

The core of our faith is summarized in the historic orthodox creeds of the early Christian church: *The Apostles' Creed, The Nicene Creed, The Athanasian Creed,* and *The Definition of Chalcedon*. We also affirm broadly the major confessions of faith of the Protestant Reformation, especially *The Canons of Dort* and *The Westminster Confession of Faith & Catechisms,* and fully subscribe to *The London Baptist Confession of Faith of 1689*. We have "a goodly heritage" (Psalm 16:6).

The ultimate goal of Veritas Heritage Press is to glorify the triune God of Holy Scripture by engaging the average person in the pew or on the street with the divinely revealed truths of this God. Our secondary goal, in this day of theological and moral decline, is to revive biblical churchmanship in evangelical Christianity, and our third goal is the conversion of sinners through the gospel. In keeping with these goals, the books will be written in a popular and simple style, accessible to all, instead of aiming at the high "groves of academia."

Because it is the most familiar and commonly used among all English-speaking peoples, the Authorized Version (King James Version) will be used for all Scripture verses. Exceptions will be made when the Old Testament Hebrew, the New Testament Greek, or a modern version gives a clearer translation. Manuscripts may be submitted to the Editorial Board.

Veritas Heritage Press
173 Brook Hill Court
Elkin, NC 28621
www.VeritasHeritagePress.com

# NOTES

# NOTES